WHSmith

Handwriting Workbook 2

English

Practice — *Reinforces classroom s[kills]*

Handwriting
WORKBOOK 2

+ Extra practice for all of the key curriculum topics
+ Written by teachers

Practice
Challenge
Progress Tests
Revision
National Test Practice Papers

**Age 5–7
Years 1–2
Key Stage 1**

Hachette UK's policy is to use papers that are natural, renewable and recyclable products and made from wood grown in sustainable forests. The logging and manufacturing processes are expected to conform to the environmental regulations of the country of origin.

Orders: please contact Bookpoint Ltd, 130 Milton Park, Abingdon, Oxon OX14 4SB. Telephone: (44) 01235 827720. Fax: (44) 01235 400454. Lines are open 9.00a.m.–5.00p.m., Monday to Saturday, with a 24-hour message answering service. Visit our website at www.hoddereducation.co.uk.

© Gill Budgell of Frattempo Ltd 2013
First published in 2013 exclusively for WHSmith by
Hodder Education
An Hachette UK Company
338 Euston Road
London NW1 3BH

Impression number   10 9 8 7 6 5 4 3 2
Year   2018 2017 2016 2015 2014

This edition has been updated, 2014, to reflect National Curriculum changes.

All rights reserved. Apart from any use permitted under UK copyright law, no part of this publication may be reproduced or transmitted in any form or by any means, electronic or mechanical, including photocopying and recording, or held within any information storage and retrieval system, without permission in writing from the publisher or under licence from the Copyright Licensing Agency Limited. Further details of such licences (for reprographic reproduction) may be obtained from the Copyright Licensing Agency Limited, Saffron House, 6–10 Kirby Street, London EC1N 8TS.

Cover illustration by Oxford Designers and Illustrators Ltd
Illustrations by Phoenix Photosetting, Chatham, Kent
Typeset in 18pt Folio BT by Phoenix Photosetting, Chatham Kent
Printed in Italy

A catalogue record for this title is available from the British Library.

ISBN: 978 1444 188 110

Advice for parents

All literacy work in schools follows the National Curriculum for English in which reading, writing and spoken language are all a focus. This series of books aims to support the work your child does at school.

Writing includes spelling and handwriting skills (transcription) and talking about ideas and structuring them in writing (composition).

Handwriting skills

Pattern practice is an important part of developing your child's handwriting skills.

When you focus on letter joining with your child ask:

- Where does the letter start?
- Is it a joining letter?
- Does it join with a diagonal or a horizontal join?
- Does it join diagonally? (ai, un)
- Does it join diagonally into an ascender? (it, ab)
- Does it join diagonally into an 'up and over'? (into: a, c, d, g, o, q, s)
- Does it join horizontally? (ou, wi)
- Does it join horizontally into an ascender? (ol, wh)
- Does it join horizontally into an 'up and over'? (after: o, r, v and w; into: a, c, d, g, o, q, s)
- Is it a break letter? (g, j, x, y, z)

The book is designed for children to complete individually, but you may like to work with them for the first few pages to check they are happy with reading the questions. They can work through the book unit by unit, or they can dip in and out to practise a particular skill.

The Practice Workbook range is easy to use as stand-alone workbooks. They also complement the Practice series, which is full of explanations and examples. If your child is finding something tricky, you may like to look at the corresponding Practice title to help reinforce and improve their understanding.

By the end of Year 2, most children should be able to:

- write legibly, using upper and lower case letters appropriately within words, and observing correct spacing within and between words;
- form and use the four basic handwriting joins;
- join into a, c, d, g, o, q, s;
- know when not to join;
- write legible numbers with correct size, spacing and orientation;
- use spacing between words that reflects the size of the letters.

See pages 46–47 for more information about pencil hold, posture and paper position.

1: Practising the four letter formations (1)

Activity 1

Copy each letter in the next spaces on the ladder.

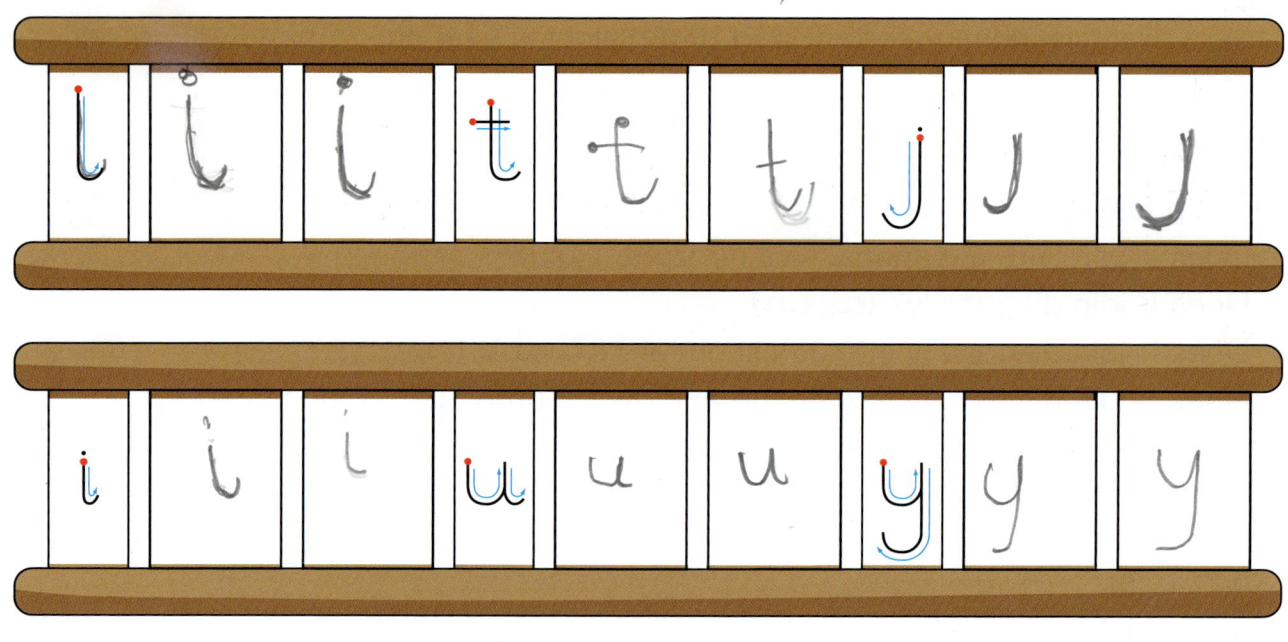

Trace the letters with your pencil. Now you write the letters.

Activity 2

Copy each letter in the next space of the robot's arm.

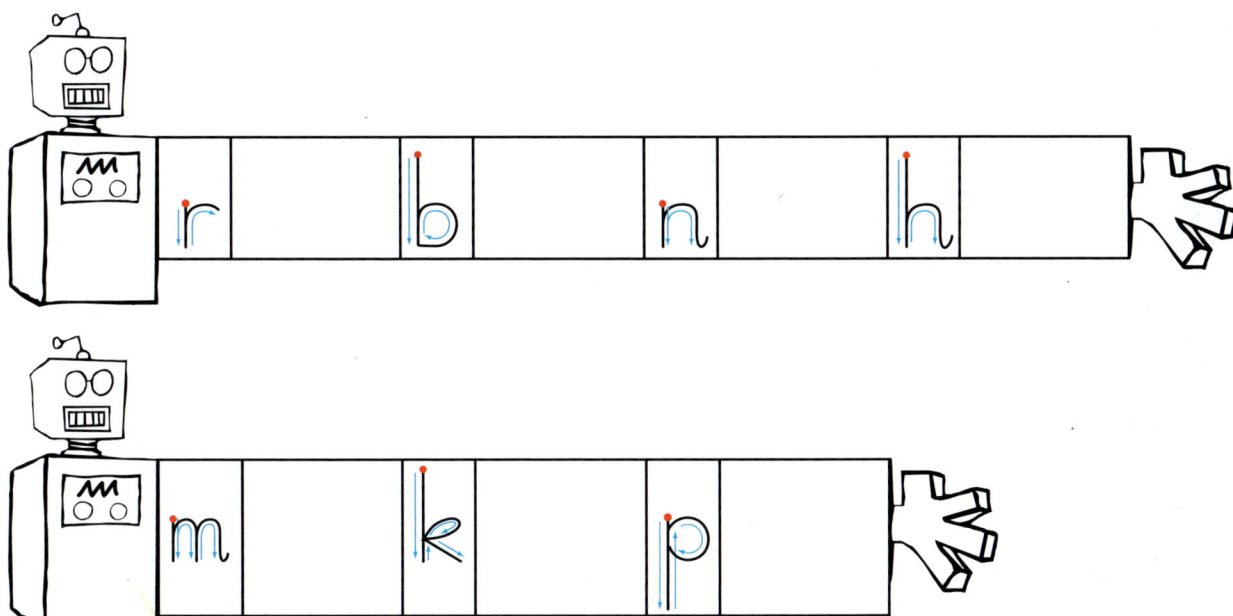

Trace the letters with your pencil. Now you write the letters.

n m n m

r m r m

b h b h

k p k p

2: Practising the four letter formations (2)

Activity 1

Copy each letter in the next space of the caterpillar.

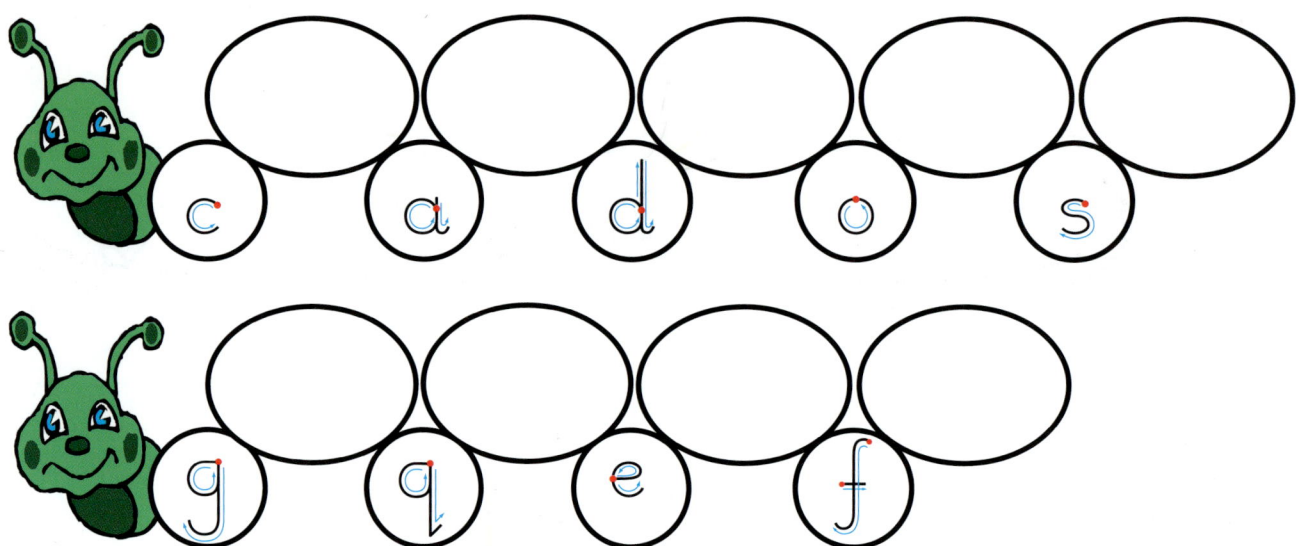

Trace the letters with your pencil. Now you write the letters.

Activity 2

Copy each letter in the next space of the zigzag path.

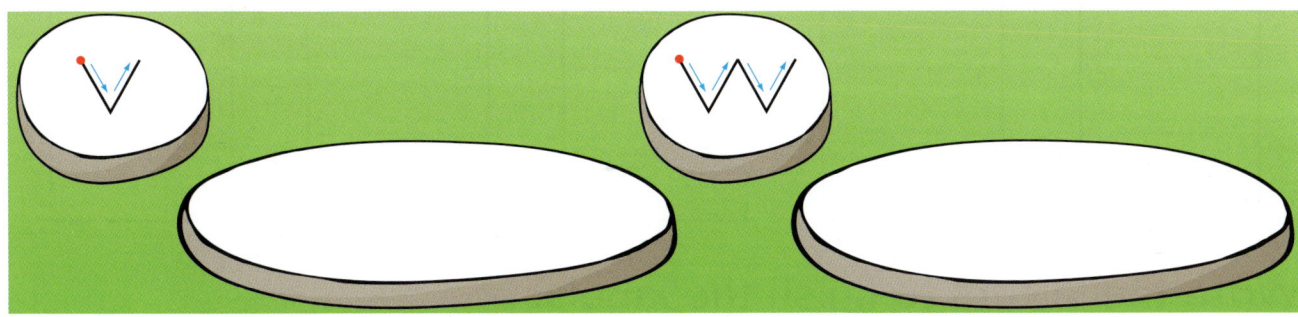

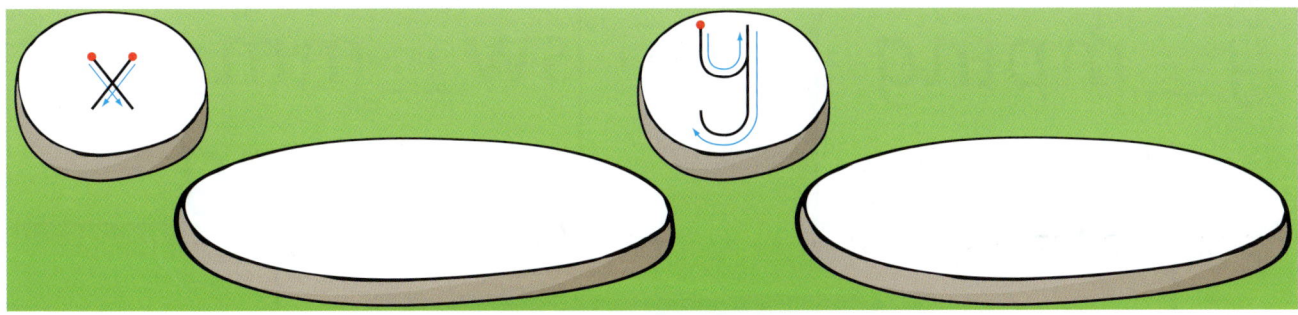

Trace the letters with your pencil. Now you write the letters.

Which letter do you find the trickiest to write? Write a line of that letter.

_____

3: Practising vowels

Activity 1

Trace the letters with your pencil. Say each letter sound. Say each letter name.

a e i o u

Write the letters to finish the labels.

j_mping _n

sw_mm_ng r_ng

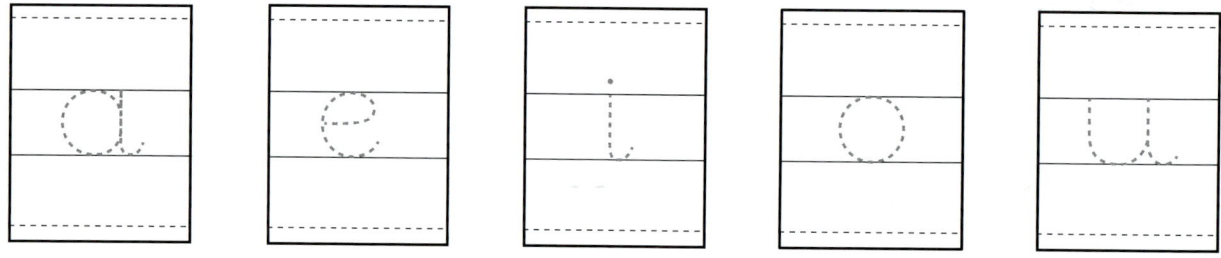

g_ggl_s

armb_nds

r_d tr_nks

8

Activity 2

Write the words for these pictures.

1 　　2

_____　　_____

3 　　4

_____　　_____

Sort these letters into words.　　Write the finished words here.

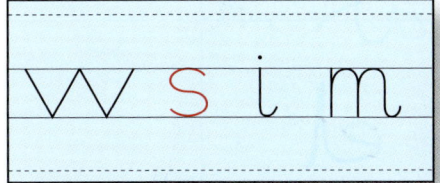　　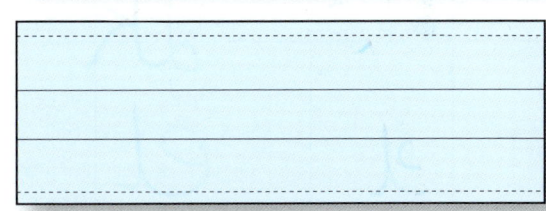

　　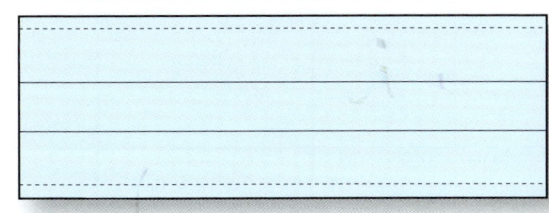

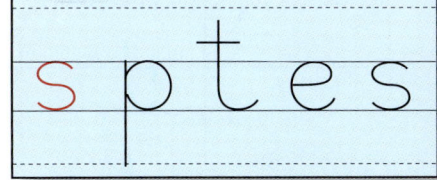　　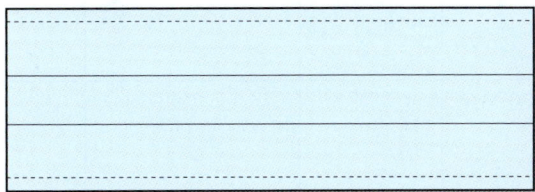

4: Practising capital letters (1)

Activity 1

Trace the letters with your pencil. Say each letter sound and each letter name.

Practise writing the capital letter twice.

Then trace the names with your pencil. Read each name and draw a picture of the person.

Lower case letter	Capital	Practice 1	Practice 2	Name	Picture
a	A			Adam	
b	B			Ben	
c	C			Cat	
d	D			Dan	
e	E			Ellen	
f	F			Fred	
g	G			Gita	

Activity 2

Trace the letters with your pencil. Say each letter sound and each letter name.

Practise writing the capital letter twice.

Then trace the names with your pencil. Read each name and draw a picture of the person.

Lower case letter	Capital	Practice 1	Practice 2	Name	Picture
h	H			Helen	
i	I			India	
j	J			Jack	
k	K			Katy	
l	L			Lola	
m	M			Matt	
n	N			Nadeem	

5: Practising capital letters (2)

Activity 1

Trace the letters with your pencil. Say each letter sound and each letter name.

Practise writing the capital letter twice.

Then trace the names with your pencil. Read each name and draw a picture of the person.

Lower case letter	Capital	Practice 1	Practice 2	Name	Picture
o	O			Olga	
p	P			Poppy	
q	Q			Queen	
r	R			Raz	
s	S			Sam	
t	T			Tilly	
u	U			Unwin	

Activity 2

Trace the letters with your pencil. Say each letter sound and each letter name.

Practise writing the capital letter twice.

Then trace the names with your pencil. Read each name and draw a picture of the person.

Lower case letter	Capital	Practice 1	Practice 2	Name	Picture
v	V			Vaz	
w	W			Will	
x	X			Max	
y	Y			Yazi	
z	Z			Zoe	

6: Joining patterns (1) – diagonal joins

Activity 1

Trace the letters with your pencil.

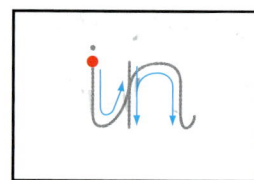

Trace the letters with your pencil. Say the sound.

Write the joining letters across the page.

Match the join to the picture. Write the join to finish each word.

ie	_____		tie
ur	_____		c__l
er	_____		ladd__
ay	_____		tr__
air	_____		h__

Activity 2

Trace the letters with your pencil. Say each sound.

Write the joining letters across the page.

Match the join to the picture. Write the join to finish each word.

7: Joining patterns – diagonal joins into ascenders

16/3/18

Activity 1

Trace the letters with your pencil.

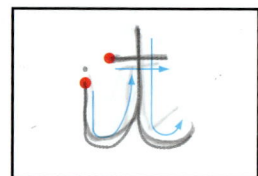

Join each red letter with each blue letter.
Finish the chart.

	b	h	k	l	t
a	ab	ab	ab	ab	ab
c	ch	ch	ch	ch	ch
d	dk	dk	dk	dk	dk
e	el	el	el	el	el
h	hk	hk	hk	hk	hk
i	it	it	it	it	it

16/3/18.

Activity 2

Trace the letters with your pencil.

Write the missing joins to make the words.

	b	h	k	l	t
a	tab		yak	play	
c		cat	chick	clip	act
e	web			eek	bet
i	bib			tilt	pit

Trace and then copy these sentences.

Jack and Jill went up the hill.

Jack and Jill went up the hill.

I like chicken and chips.

I like chicken and chips.

8: Joining patterns (1) – practising mixed diagonal joins

Activity 1

Trace the letters with your pencil.

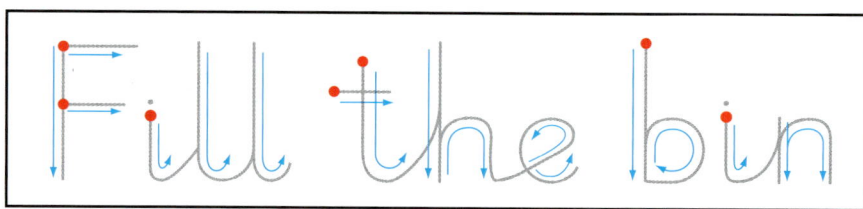

Trace the letters with your pencil. Then finish the patterns.

Activity 2

Join the letters and write the words.

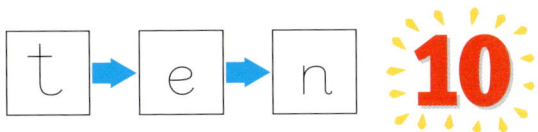 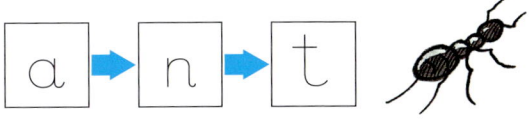

_____   _____

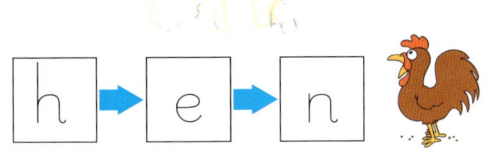

_____

Trace these words with a pencil. Now you write them.

Jack _____ Jill _____ _____

went _____ up _____ _____

hill _____ chips _____ _____

and _____ like _____ _____

9: Joining patterns (1) – horizontal joins to a, c, d, g, o, q, s

Activity 1

Trace the letters with your pencil.

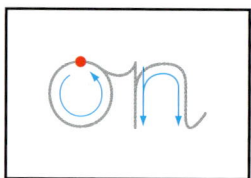

Trace the letters with your pencil. Say the sound.

Write the joining letters across the page.

Match the join to the picture. Write the join to finish each word.

oe _____   toe

or _____   f__k

ow _____   b__

oi _____   c__n

oy _____   b__

20

Activity 2

Trace the letters with your pencil. Say the sound.

Write the joining letters across the page.

Match the join to the picture. Write the join to finish each word.

vi ———————— view

ve ———————— __st

we ———————— cob__b

wi ———————— __ndow

10: Joining patterns (1) – practising horizontal joins to ascenders

Activity 1

Trace the letters with your pencil.

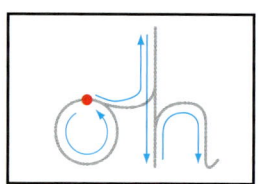

Join each red letter with each blue letter.
Finish the chart.

	b	h	k	l	t
o	ob				
v		vh			vt
w			wk		

Join each red letter with each blue letter.
Write the missing joins to make the words.

	b	h	k	l	t
o	sob	___	__ay	__d	h__
w		__at		o__	

22

Activity 2

Trace the letters with your pencil.

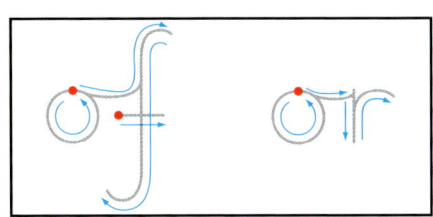

Join each red letter with each blue letter.

Finish the chart.

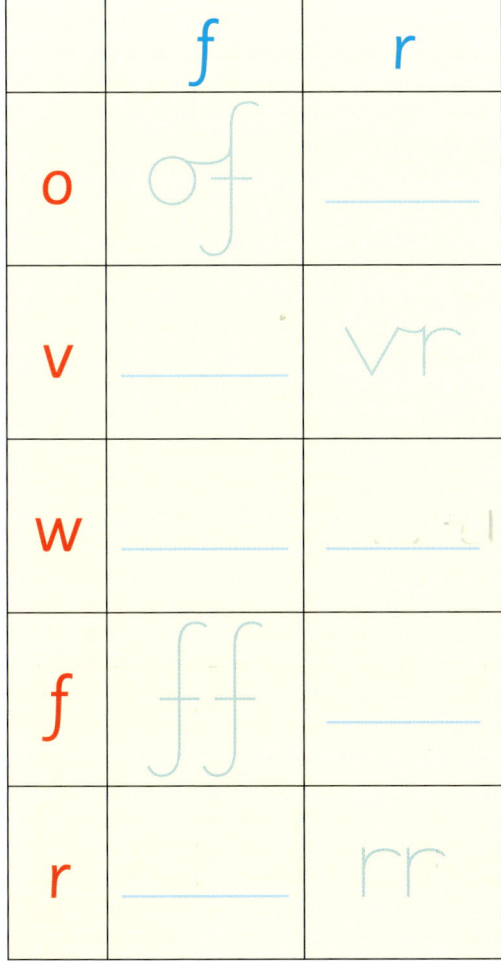

Join each red letter with each blue letter.

Write the missing joins to make the words.

	f	r
o	___	f___
w		___ap
f	o___	___og
r	sca___	

11: Joining patterns (2) – practising mixed horizontal joins

Activity 1

Trace the letters with your pencil.

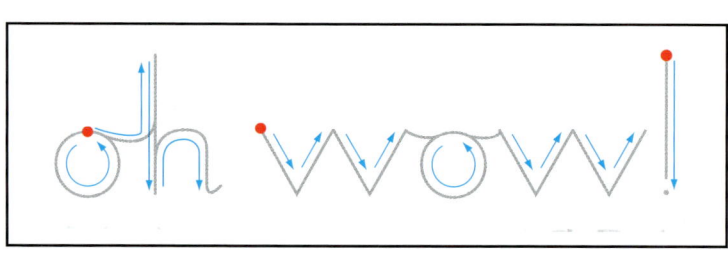

Trace the letters with your pencil. Then write these letter patterns yourself.

ohoh ohoh

wvwv wvwv

ftft ftft

whwh whwh

riri riri

fefe fefe

Activity 2

Join the letters and write the words.

o → n → e 　1　　f → i → n

_____　　　_____

w → h → e → n

_____

Trace these words with a pencil. Now you write the letters.

what _____　　toy _____

box   _____　　old _____

red   _____　　soft _____

one   _____　　cow _____

Trace and then copy this sentence.

Hey, what is in the toy box? _____

_____

12: Joining patterns (2) – diagonal joins to a, c, d, g, o, q, s

Activity 1

Trace the letters with your pencil.

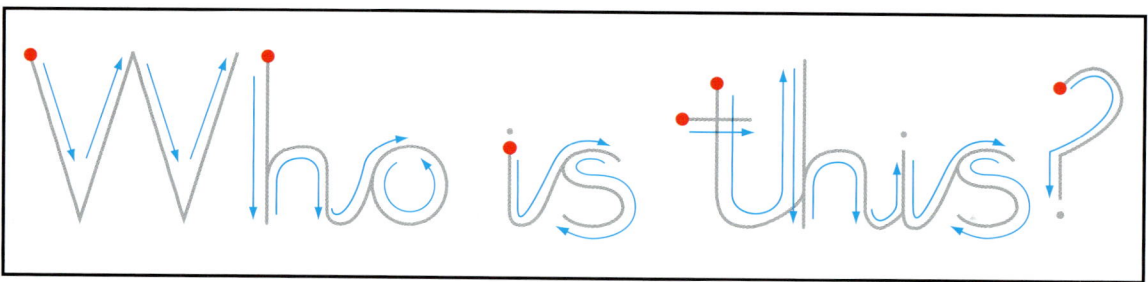

Join each red letter with each blue letter.

Finish the chart.

Remember to go 'up and over' to join into these letters!

	a	c	o	s	d	g	q
e				es			
h		hc					
i							
k						kg	
l			lo				
m							mq
n							
t	ta						
u					ud		

26

Activity 2

Trace the words with your pencil to label the picture.

head   mosquito   ear

nose   eyes

face

mouth

tongue

13: Joining patterns (2) – horizontal joins to a, c, d, g, o, g, s

● **Activity 1**

Trace the letters with your pencil.

Join each red letter with each blue letter. Finish the chart.
Remember to go 'up and over' to join into these letters!

	a	c	o	s	d	g	q
o	oa						
f				fs			
r							rq
v		vc					
w					wd		

 **Activity 2**

Trace the words with your pencil.
Join each picture to the right words.

   dog in a boat

horse on a farm

vole on the road

   worm in the forest

rat in a vase

   hippos in water

14: Joining patterns (2) – joining from vowels

Activity 1

Trace the letters with your pencil.

Write the joining letters across the page.

Match the join to the picture. Write the join to finish each word.

ai	———————	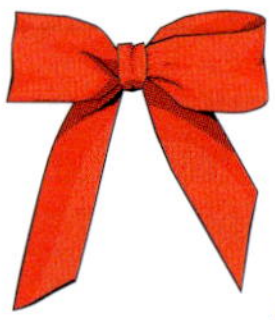	tail
ea	———————	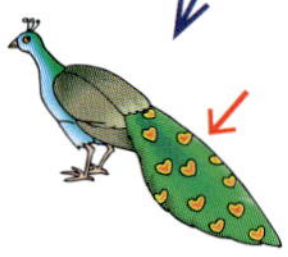	s__
igh	———————	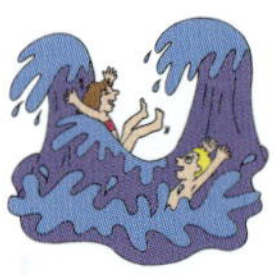	l__t
ow	———————	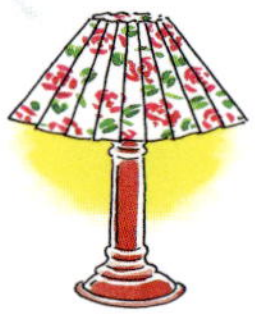	b__
ue	———————	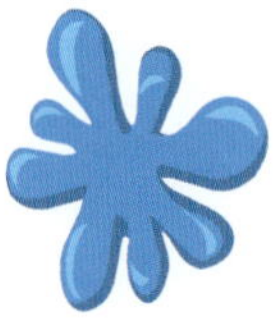	bl__

Activity 2

Trace the letters with your pencil. Write the letters to finish the words and label the picture.

Use these letters to help you: **igh**, **ea**, **ue**, **ow**, **ai**.

My bl__ and yell__ bike

yell__

p__nt

l__t

s__t

bl__

p__nt

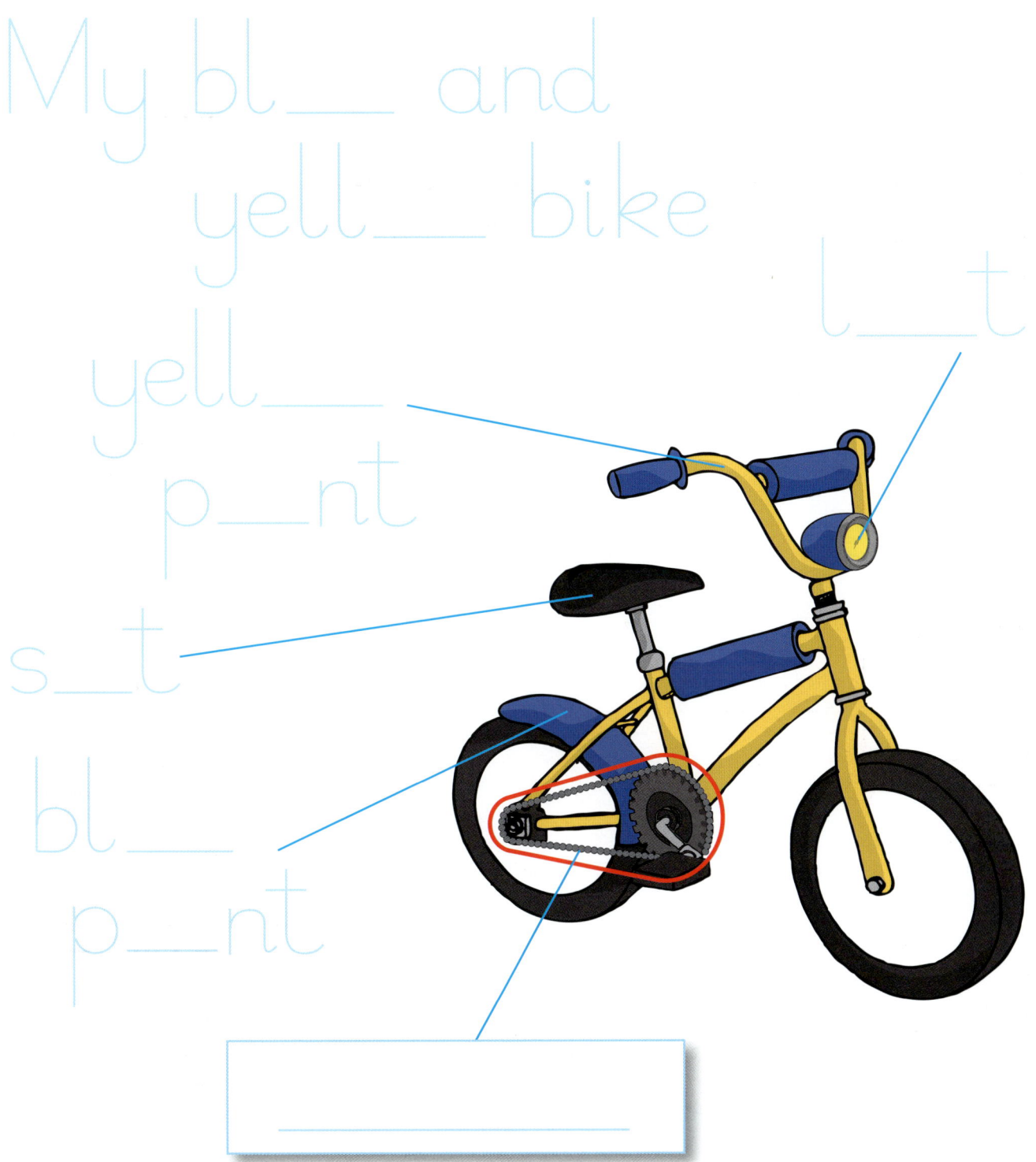

15: Joining patterns (2) – practising joining nk, ch, sh, th, wh, ck

Activity 1

Trace the letters with your pencil.

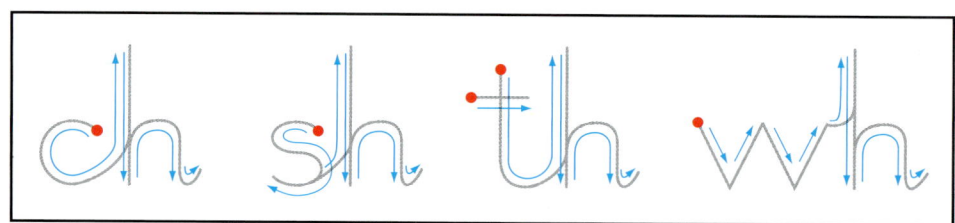

Trace and then write the letters and words.

ch sh _____ _____

chatty children _____ _____

shiny shells _____ _____

th wh _____ _____

three things _____ _____

white whale _____ _____

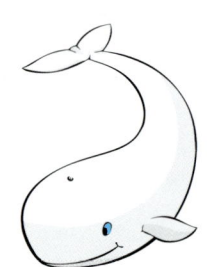

Activity 2

Trace the letters with your pencil.

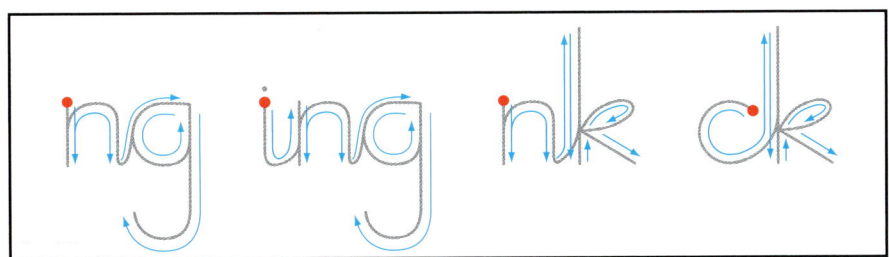

Write the joining letters across the page.

Match the join to the picture. Write the join to finish each word.

16: Joining patterns (2) – practising joining double letters

Activity 1

Trace the letters with your pencil.

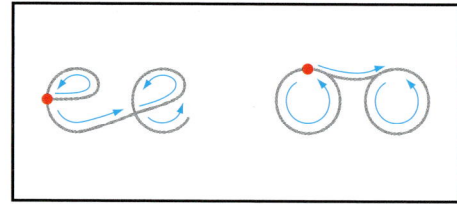

Trace the letters with a pencil. Say the sound. Now you write them.

ee ee _____

oo oo _____

Trace and then copy these words.

three bees looking

_____

at books

Activity 2

Trace the letters with your pencil.

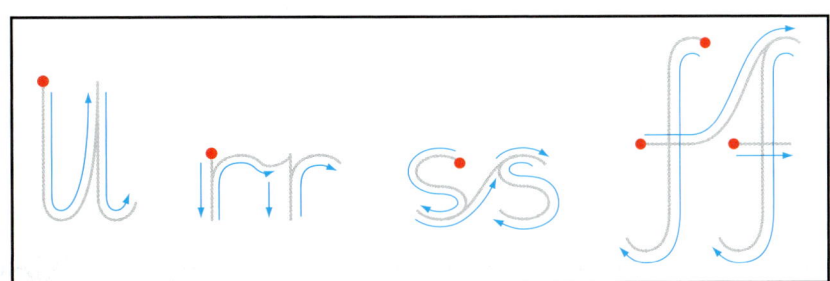

Write the joining letters across the page.

Match the join to the picture. Write the join to finish each word.

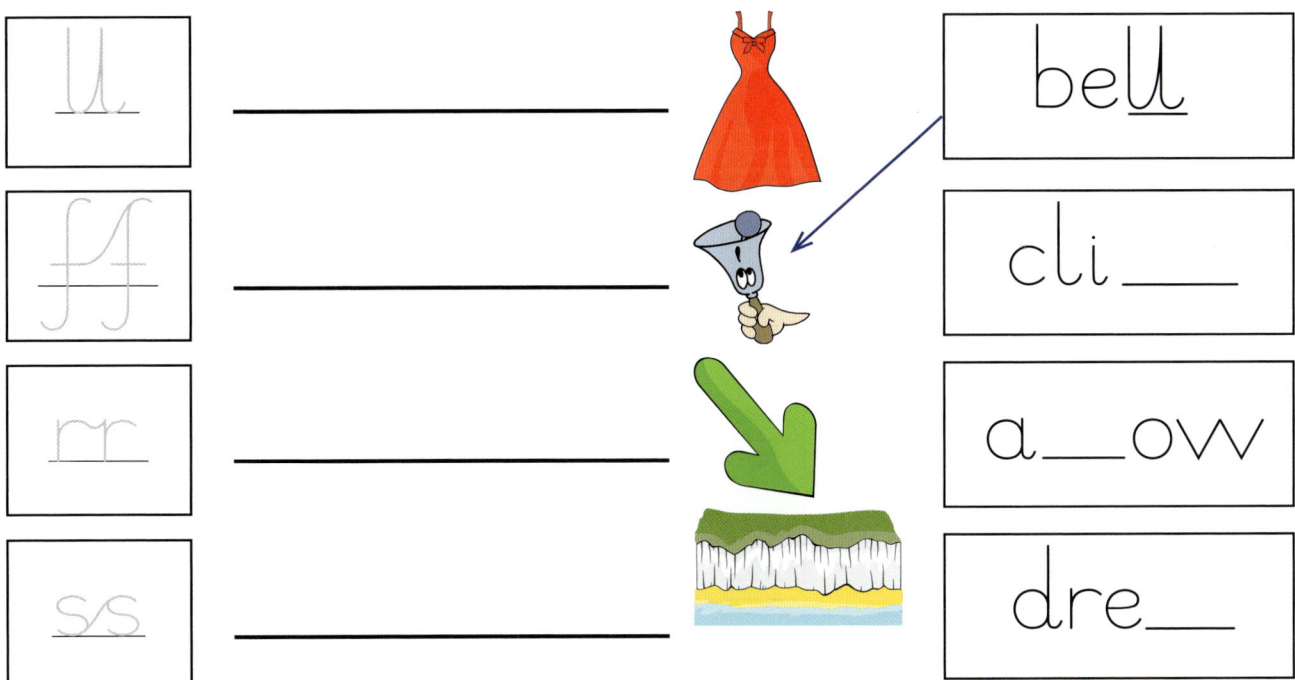

Write each word again. Join as many letters as you can.

17: Joining patterns (2) – no joins

Activity 1

Trace the letters with your pencil.

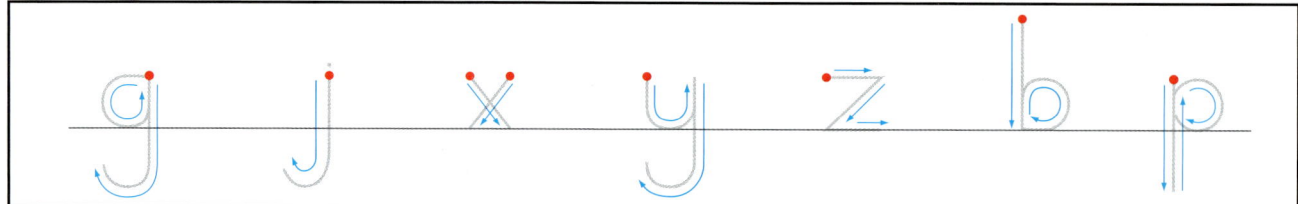

Read each word. Join **to** each red letter but not **from** it.
Trace each word. Write it yourself.

	Read	Trace	Write
g	night	night	_____
j	jeans	jeans	_____
x	foxes	foxes	_____
y	eye	eye	_____
z	quizzes	quizzes	_____
b	rabbit	rabbit	_____
p	sleeping	sleeping	_____

36

Activity 2

Join the letters and write the words. Think about which letters to join.

z ➔ a ➔ p _____

b ➔ e ➔ g _____

p ➔ u ➔ p ➔ s _____

b ➔ a ➔ b ➔ y _____

Trace the letters with your pencil. Read each phrase.

yelling yetis

skipping pixies

juggling foxes

zooming robbers

18: Joined-up writing – tricky bits, tips and rules

Activity 1

Join the letters and write the words. Be careful with the tricky bits!

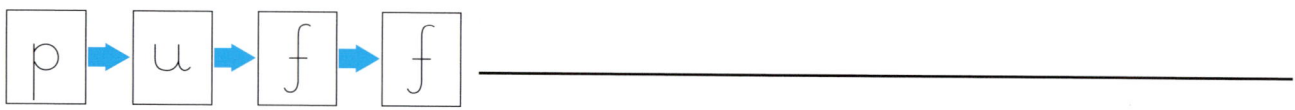 puff

 offer

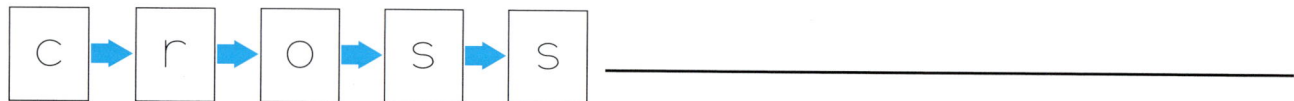 cross

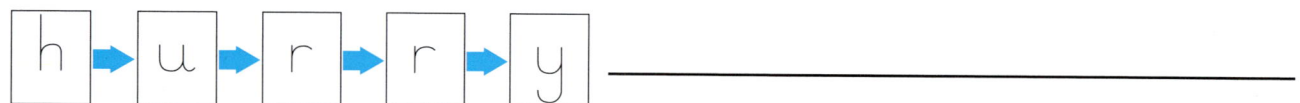 hurry

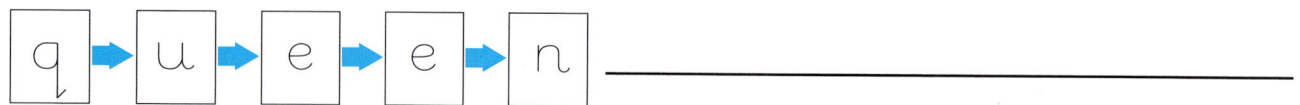 queen

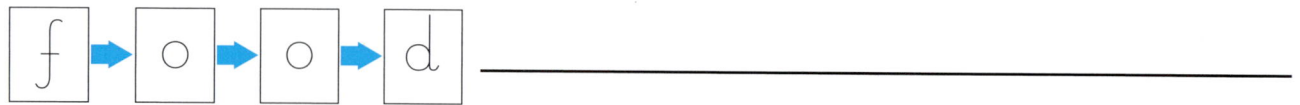 food

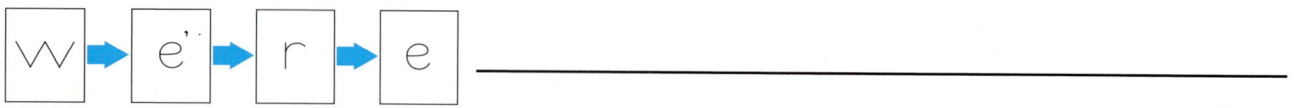 we're

Trace and copy these sentences.

Handwriting tips and rules

1. Keep letters the same size.

2. Go up, over and back to join a, c, d, g, o, q and s.

3. Don't join from g, j, x, y, z, b and p.

4. Don't join CAPITAL LETTERS.

5. Keep descenders the same length.

6. Keep ascenders the same height.

19: Joined-up writing words – common words and tricky bits

Activity 1

Write each word without joining. Then write each word joined.

Common words	Not joined	Joined
as	as	as
if		
is		
up		
can		
dad		
back		
mum		
and		
get		
but		
will		
with		
see		
for		
now		
look		
down		
just		

Activity 2

Write the joins. Then write the whole words.

Tricky words	Join th, wh, ch, sh, kn	Write the word
the	th	the
that		
this		
then		
them		
with		
they		
there		
when		
what		
their		
children		
where		
school		
know		
shouted		
through		
something		
much		

20: Joined-up writing words – numbers and colours

Activity 1

Write the numbers and words.

		Number	Word
1	one	1	one
2	two		
3	three		
4	four		
5	five		
6	six		
7	seven		
8	eight		
9	nine		
10	ten		

How are you doing? Look at your writing above with an adult.

	Check	Yes	No
1	Are the letters formed correctly?		
2	Are the numbers formed correctly?		
3	Are the small letters the same size?		
4	Are the letters sitting on the line?		
5	Are the ascenders (letters that are tall) above the line?		
6	Are the descenders (letters with tails) below the line?		
7	Are the diagonal joins correct?		
8	Are the horizontal joins correct?		
9	Have you <u>not</u> joined from **g** in eight?		
10	Is the writing clear and easy to read?		

Activity 2

Write the letters and words.

		Letters	Word
R	red	r e d	red
B	blue		
Y	yellow		
G	green		
P	pink		
BL	black		
BR	brown		
PU	purple		
W	white		

How are you doing? Look at your writing above with an adult.

	Check	Yes	No
1	Are the capital letters formed correctly?		
2	Are the small letters formed correctly?		
3	Are the small letters the same size?		
4	Are the letters sitting on the line?		
5	Are the ascenders (letters that are tall) above the line?		
6	Are the descenders (letters with tails) below the line?		
7	Are the diagonal joins correct?		
8	Are the horizontal joins correct?		
9	Have you not joined from **b**, **p** and **g**?		
10	Is the writing clear and easy to read?		

21: Joined-up writing words – days of the week and checklist

Activity 1

Write the words yourself.

My weekly plan	
Monday	
Tuesday	
Wednesday	
Thursday	
Friday	
Saturday	
Sunday	

How are you doing? Look at your writing above with an adult.

	Check	Yes	No
1	Are the letters formed correctly?		
2	Are the small letters the same size?		
3	Are the letters sitting on the line?		
4	Are the ascenders (letters that are tall) above the line?		
5	Are the descenders (letters that have a tail) below the line?		
6	Are the capital letters not joined and the same height as ascenders?		
7	Are the diagonal joins correct?		
8	Are the horizontal joins correct?		
9	Have you not joined from the capitals and **p** in plan?		
10	Is the writing clear and easy to read?		

Summary of joins

Join	Join letters in this box	To letters in this box
Diagonal join	a c d e h l k l m n q s t u	e l j m n p r u v w y
Diagonal join to ascender	a c d e h l k l m n s t u	b f h k l t
Up and over from a diagonal	a c d e h l k l m n q s t u	a c d g o q s
Horizontal join	f o r v w	e l j m n p r u v w y
Horizontal join to ascender	f o r v w	b f h k l t
Up and over from a horizontal	f o r v w	a c d g o q s
Break letters: join **to** but not **from** these letters	g j x y z b p	–

*Some school handwriting programmes teach joining of all letters. Some include joining of **b** and **p**.

Paper position

Paper position for right-handers

Paper position for left-handers